We Are Extraordinary
ISBN 978-0-993077388

First published in 2019 in the United Kingdom.

This version was first published by
Fisherton Press in 2020.

Text © Eleanor Levenson 2019
Illustrations © Farah Ishaq 2019

A CIP catalogue record for this book is
available from the British Library.

The right of Eleanor Levenson to be identified
as the author of this work has been asserted
by her in accordance with the Copyrights,
Designs and Patents Act, 1988.

The right of Farah Ishaq to be identified as the
illustrator of this work has been asserted
by her in accordance with the Copyrights,
Designs and Patents Act, 1988

We Are Extraordinary

WORDS BY ELEANOR LEVENSON
PICTURES BY FARAH ISHAQ

Introduction

In 1992, when I was 14, shortly after the beginning of the academic year, I was on the bus from my school in Chingford to my home in Walthamstow. A friend and I were looking at a copy of *Smash Hits*, a pop music magazine. It had a list of things that were 'hot' that week, and things that were 'not'. On the 'not' list was the city of Seattle, home to a type of music called grunge, and on the 'hot' list was Walthamstow. A new band had a single out. They were called East 17, after the postcode of where we lived. Better yet, we looked up and on our very bus was an actual member of East 17, whose picture was in the magazine on our laps.

Whether you liked them or not – and they were both very successful and the object of much ridicule – that moment of seeing our town on the cool list in a magazine was brilliant. I even cut it out and stuck it on my bedroom wall. It was a reminder that our ordinary lives need not always be this way, and that ordinary people from ordinary towns can do completely extraordinary things.

Waltham Forest is an amazing borough. Look in one direction and you see into the vast swathes of Epping Forest and all the magic (and fear) that the forest can bring, from picnics and den building to real life historic highwaymen and imagined goblins and fairies.

Look in another direction and you can see the gleam of towers at Docklands. Swivel round and you see the recognisable

shapes of buildings in the City of London.

And just a stone's throw away, visible from the many hills of the borough, the modern architecture of the Queen Elizabeth Olympic Park, a reminder that hard work and dedication can push the human body to its very limits, and that countries can come together in celebration of all that can be achieved.

One of the great things about London is that anyone can arrive here from anywhere in the world and if they love London then London will love them back. You do not have to be born in London to be a Londoner. That is why this book includes people who have worked here, those who have studied here, and those who only lived here temporarily, as well as those who have spent their whole lives in Waltham Forest.

The people in this book are ordinary people from an ordinary place. They walked down your streets, lived in your houses and played in your parks. They went to your schools and shopped in your shops. They are ordinary. But they are extraordinary too, creating art and music that inspires, excelling at sport and changing the world though inventions and ideas. They are extraordinary and you too are extraordinary.

We are extraordinary.

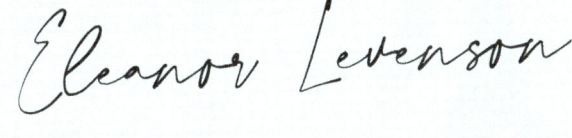

The List

Sport

Beryl Swain
1936-2007

Nasser Hussain
born 1968

Lutalo Muhammad
born 1991

Roy Romain
1918-2010

Laurie Cunningham
1956-1989

Jade Bailey
born 1995

Bobby Moore
1941-1993

David Beckham
born 1975

Harry Kane
born 1993

Science & Invention

Vincent Crane Richmond
1893-1930

George Edwards
1908-2003

Edwin Alliott Verdon-Roe
1877-1958

Louisa Aldrich-Blake
1865-1925

Edward Atkinson
1881-1929

Morell Mackenzie
1837-1892

John Kemp Starley
1854-1901

Frederick Bremer
1872-1941

Harry Beck
1902-1974

Fanny Cradock
1909 – 1994

Social Change

Jenny Hammond
1894 - 1988

Ada Maddocks
1927-2007

Benjamin Disraeli
1804-1881

Clement Attlee
1883-1967

Stella Creasy
born 1977

Patricia Scotland
born 1955

Thomas Gamuel
died c 1643

George Monoux
c 1465 – 1544

Edward Lloyd
1815 - 1890

Sol Plaatje
1876 – 1932

Muriel Lester
1883 – 1968

Jack Cornwell
1900-1916

George Mitchell
1911 – 1944

Patrick Mullane
1858-1919

Edgar Myles
1894 – 1977

Creativity

Stuart Freeborn
1914 – 2013

Alfred Hitchcock
1899 – 1980

Derek Jacobi
born 1938

Marion Foale
born 1939

Sally Tuffin
born 1938

David Bailey
born 1938

Matthew Bourne
born 1960

Roger Ascham
c 1515 – 1568

George Gascoigne
c 1535 – 1577

Tom Hood
1835 – 1874

Thomas Hood
1799 – 1845

Madge Gill
1882 – 1961

Grayson Perry
born 1960

William Morris
1834 – 1896

Music

Terry Coldwell
born 1974

Brian Harvey
born 1974

John Hendy
born 1971

Tony Mortimer
born 1970

Damon Albarn
born 1968

Talvin Singh
born 1970

Michael Nyman
born 1944

Jammer
born 1982

Lethal Bizzle
born 1984

Mandy Parnell
born 1968

John Dankworth
1927-2010

Jackie Free
born 1932

Kenny Wheeler
1930-2014

Kenny Clare
1929-1985

The Isle of Man, an island in the middle of the sea between England and Ireland, is known for dangerous motorcycle races around its roads. In 1962 **Beryl Swain** from Walthamstow was the first woman solo rider to compete in their TT races, riding her 50cc Itom bike around the mountainous circuit. The men who ran motorcycle racing felt so threatened by this that they introduced a minimum weight requirement for competitors, so that Beryl and other women couldn't race again – this lasted until 1978. She inspired many other women who came after her to believe that motorcycle racing could be for everyone and to have a go themselves.

Nasser Hussain was born in India and moved to the UK when he was a child. He went to school in Walthamstow where he played cricket, going on to play for Essex and then England. He was made captain of the England cricket team in 1999 and led the team for 45 Test matches over the next five years. Nasser started as a bowler until he grew so tall as a teenager that this became a problem, so he changed to being mainly a batsman. During his career he achieved over 60 centuries in top level cricket, which is when a batsman scores more than 100 runs in a single innings. Nasser was a Wisden Cricketer of the Year in 2003 and he now works as a cricket commentator and a school cricket coach.

Sport

Double Olympic medallist **Lutalo Muhammad** is a British taekwondo athlete from Walthamstow. His parents came to the UK from Zimbabwe and his dad coached him in taekwondo from early childhood. There was controversy when Lutalo was selected for the Olympic team in 2012, when the games were held in London, ahead of a competitor that many thought had more chance of winning. Lutalo proved them wrong when he won a medal. He won bronze in the 2012 Olympics and silver in the 2016 Olympics.

"I won almost every race I did," said **Roy Romain**, who represented Great Britain at the 200m breaststroke in the 1948 London Olympics, though that was one of the few races he actually lost. At one point he was both British and European champion. Roy was one of the first people to swim the modern butterfly stoke, demonstrating it at swimming pool galas around the country. He went on to work as a lawyer, though swam competitively throughout his whole life, winning World Masters Swimming competitions in his 70s and 80s.

"When times are down, keep believing, keep working hard, and things will pick up."

Harry Kane

Sport

Laurie Cunningham was the first black footballer to represent England in any of their adult teams and the first Englishman to play football for Real Madrid. At a time when racism was very common in football, he was one of the prominent black footballers who challenged this, on and off the pitch. He was known for his speed and balance and his transfer fee to Real Madrid from West Bromwich Albion was the highest the club had ever paid at the time. In a game against Barcelona, a newspaper said he "plays football like the angels" and at the end of the match the Barcelona fans gave the Real Madrid player a standing ovation. Laurie began his footballing career at Leyton Orient in the 1970s, and there is a statue of him next to the club in Coronation Gardens.

Jade Bailey is a professional footballer from Walthamstow. She started playing football when she was six years old, playing for Interwood, a local team coached and run by her uncle, and then for her school boys' team, Chapel End. She became the only female player for the Waltham Forest Under 11s team, and was made captain, but because the teams did not allow girls to join after age 11 she had a trial with Arsenal and started to train with them instead. She was part of their Women's FA Cup winning side two years running, later signing for Chelsea and then Liverpool as well as representing England at all youth levels. When London hosted the Olympics in 2012 she was chosen to hold the Olympic torch as it was carried by boat down the Thames during the opening ceremony, watched by one billion people

Harry Kane was born in Walthamstow and then moved with his family to Chingford, where he played for Ridgeway Rovers as a boy. He always supported Tottenham Hotspur, where he now plays, and he holds the record for being awarded Premier League Player of the Month the most times. In the 2018 World Cup Harry captained the England team, and also finished as the top goalscorer, winning the Golden Boot trophy.

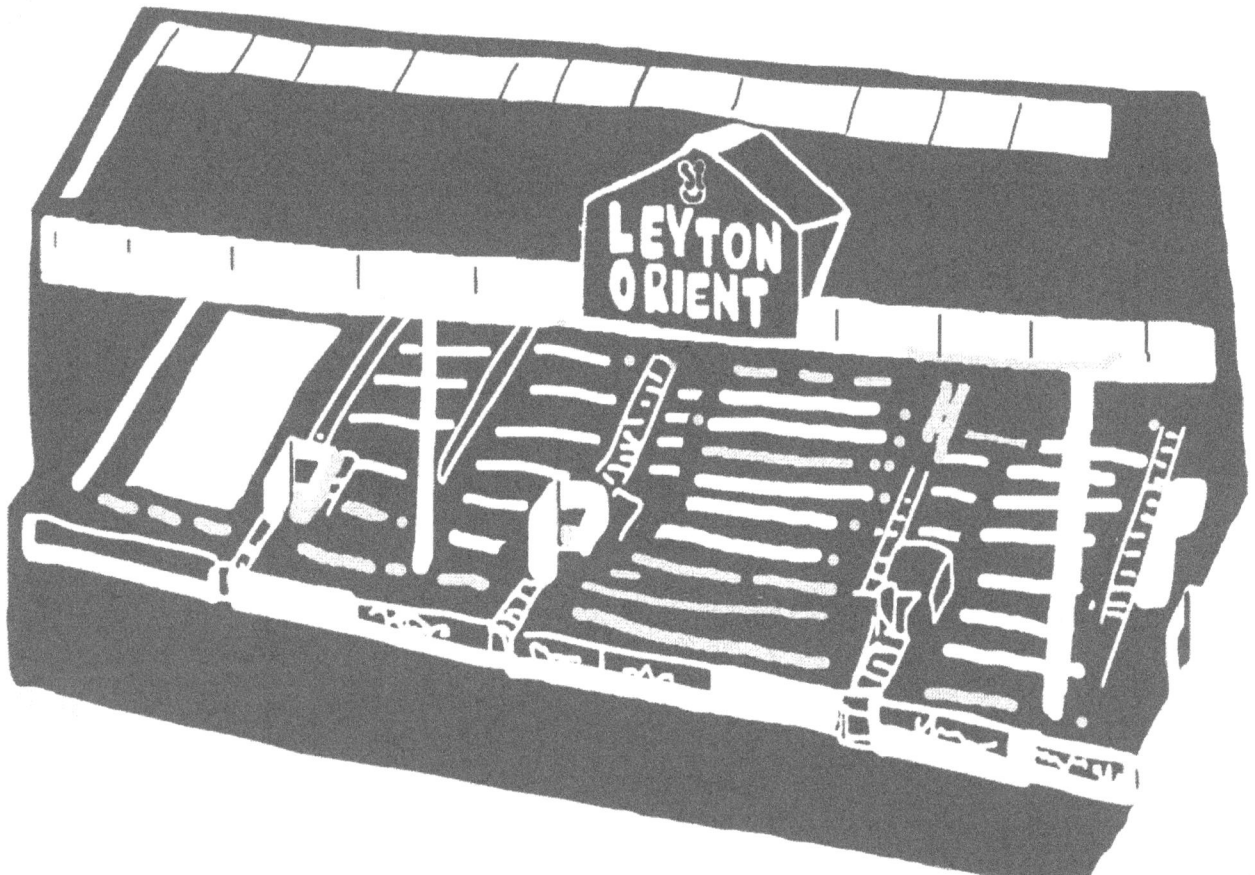

World famous footballer **David Beckham** was born in Leytonstone and went to school in Chingford, where he also played for local team Ridgeway Rovers. He captained the England football team 59 times and is the only English football player to have scored in three World Cups. He played for Manchester United, the team he grew up supporting, throughout the 1990s, and is the first English player to have won league titles in four countries - England, Spain, the United States and France. He has been in the newspapers as much for his fashion choices as his sporting skills, and has also worked with the British Fashion Council to promote British designers. He has also volunteered for many years as an ambassador for the charity UNICEF.

When England won the World Cup in 1966 the captain was **Bobby Moore**. Born in East London, he went to school in Leytonstone before signing with the youth programme at West Ham United. He is thought of as their greatest ever player and was their captain for more than 10 years as well as playing for England over 100 times. The Brazilian football superstar Pelé said he was the greatest defender he had ever played against. Bobby was the first footballer to win BBC Sports Personality of the Year. There is a statue of him outside Wembley Stadium, and one near Green Street in East London, and also a school named after him in the Olympic Park.

In the 1920s the British Government encouraged engineers to design airships that could travel long distances. Airships are cabins with huge structures filled with a gas that is lighter than air above them. **Vincent Crane Richmond** was one of the lead designers of the R101, a rigid airship that was at the time the world's largest flying machine. In October 1930 it set out on its maiden voyage (first trip), heading for India, but crashed over France killing all on board including Vincent. He lived in Highams Park as a child, where there is a road named after him.

George Edwards was born in Highams Park and went to the Walthamstow Technical Institute before studying engineering. He designed aeroplanes throughout World War Two and afterwards, working on many groundbreaking passenger aeroplanes. He was part of the team that designed Concorde, the world's first supersonic plane, which means it travelled faster than the speed of sound.

In 1909 **Edwin Alliott Verdon-Roe** became the first person to fly an aeroplane that had been made wholly in Britain, flying a triplane (an aeroplane with three pairs of wings) on Walthamstow Marshes. He became interested in building aeroplanes having watched albatrosses (large seabirds found in the Southern Hemisphere) while he was in the merchant navy. His triplane is now on display at London's Science Museum. In later years his achievements were overshadowed by his membership of the British Union of Fascists, the British equivalent of the Nazi Party.

Science & Invention

Born in 1865, **Louisa Aldrich-Blake** from Chingford was one of the first women in modern medicine to qualify as a doctor. She became a surgeon and volunteered as a military doctor during World War One as well as organising other women doctors to volunteer and persuading the War Office to allow women to join the Medical Corps. She was one of the first people to operate on certain types of cancer and was the first woman to be surgical registrar at the Royal Free Hospital as well as working in other hospitals across London.

Edward Atkinson was a doctor and explorer. Born on Saint Vincent in the West Indies and educated in Walthamstow, he was on Captain Scott's failed expedition in 1910 to be the first to the South Pole. He was in command of the base camp for much of the time after Scott died in 1912. Edward led the group that found Captain Scott's body and the diary he kept of his final days. He later went to China to research a parasite that was making British seamen ill, before serving in World War One during which he was awarded the Albert Medal for saving lives at sea.

Morell Mackenzie was a doctor from Leytonstone who specialised in laryngology, which is the study of throats. In Victorian times he also opened a throat hospital in London and wrote lots of books about this area of medicine as well as being called upon to treat members of European royal families.

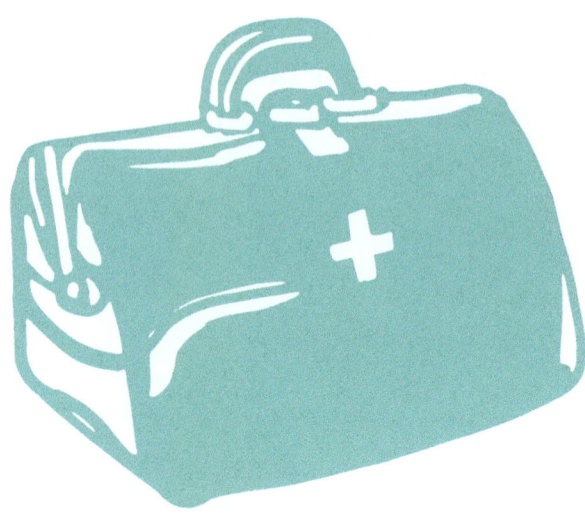

"Looking at the old map of the railways, it occurred to me that it might be possible to tidy it up by straightening the lines, experimenting with diagonals and evening out the distances between stations."

Harry Beck

Science & Invention

Phyllis Pechey was better known as **Fanny Cradock**, one of the first celebrity chefs. She wrote about restaurants and cooking for newspapers and had a television series teaching the audience how to cook European style dishes, with the recipes published in a booklet every year by the BBC. She wore ballgowns instead of aprons and tried to ensure that her recipes were affordable for most families to make. Fanny is thought to have been the person who invented the prawn cocktail, though some say she just introduced it to the UK. A prawn cocktail is essentially prawns in a 'cocktail sauce' which is usually tomato ketchup mixed with mayonnaise and some herbs or spices, served on a salad.

Before bicycles had two equally sized wheels, there were large bicycles known as Penny Farthings, with one large wheel and one small wheel. Inventor **John Kemp Starley**, who lived for the early years of his life in Walthamstow, thought that these could be made easier and safer, and came up with the design that is very similar to the bikes we ride today. He called the bicycles 'Rover', and the company he set up with a friend went on to become Rover the car manufacturer.

The first petrol-fuelled car also has a Walthamstow connection. **Frederick Bremer** worked as a gas fitter and plumber, and designed and built a four wheeled car with an internal combustion engine in 1892, which he tried out on the roads of Walthamstow. Over 73 years later in 1965 it completed the 54 mile London to Brighton car rally on its second attempt, taking just under eight hours. The car can be seen in Walthamstow's Vestry House Museum.

Every day millions of people use maps influenced by the work of Leyton born **Harry Beck**, who in 1931 created the London Underground map that is still in use today and that has been copied around the world. The map is a topological map which means it has been made simple and only contains the information you need to know, as well as not being to scale. Harry worked for London Underground in a different job but came up with the map in his spare time. Nowadays every London Underground map has a statement on it recognising that Harry came up with the original design.

Social Change

Jenny Hammond was born in Leyton and was a local Labour Party councillor for many years. She was elected for the first time in 1929 and as a councillor she helped introduce many things to make people's lives better, from public baths at a time when people did not have baths in their houses, to health clinics for those who needed them. She tried to ensure that people who did not have much money got what they needed to be able to live their lives. Jenny achieved change even before she was elected – during the General Strike in 1926 when people across the country stopped working in support of coalminers who were being asked to work for low wages in bad conditions, she protested at Leyton Town Hall to ensure the babies of people on strike were given the milk they needed. Jenny was a Mayor of the Borough of Leyton in 1942-43 (this is now part of the Borough of Waltham Forest) and Chair of their education committee for many years. There is now a school in Leytonstone named after her.

Trade Unions are organisations that bring workers in the same type of job together to improve their working conditions. One of the leading women in this movement was **Ada Maddocks**. She spent many years working for a Trade Union called Nalgo (National Association of Local Government Officers), and by the end of her career she was President of the TUC (Trades Union Congress) which represents many Trade Unions. When ambulance workers were on strike while she was president of the TUC, she worked hard to ensure people in other types of work supported them. The meat porters at Smithfield Market were so impressed with her that early one morning they let her stand on one of their barrows – something they had only ever let royalty do before this. Ada was born in Suffolk but grew up in Walthamstow where she also went to school. People who worked with her remarked that she was particularly encouraging to them in their own careers, helping them to achieve the most that they could and to be promoted.

Social Change

Benjamin Disraeli served as Prime Minister twice, briefly in 1868 and again 1874-1880. He spent some time as a child going to a school on Higham Hill in Walthamstow. Benjamin called himself a 'one-nation conservative' and he thought that ordinary people should be looked after by the government and that people should work towards the good of all society. Laws passed while he was Prime Minister the first time ended public executions, and laws passed when he was Prime Minister for the second time banned child chimney sweeps and ensured people had running water and that their rubbish was collected. He was also a writer, publishing several novels and other books, and is the only British Prime Minister so far who was born Jewish, although he became a Christian aged 12. He is not the only Prime Minister with Walthamstow connections however. **Clement Attlee** was Prime Minister from 1945-1950. He later represented Walthamstow West as its Member of Parliament (MP) from 1951-1955. It was his government that created the National Health Service (NHS).

Since 2010 the Member of Parliament (MP) for Walthamstow has been **Stella Creasy**. She has campaigned for stronger rules for loan companies, working to make sure people are not made poorer by the companies lending them money. Stella is a strong campaigner for women's rights, including working with MPs from other parties to ensure that women from Northern Ireland have access to the same medical services as women in the rest of the UK, and she helped to make misogyny (hatred directed towards women) a hate crime, speaking out in particular against those who send horrible messages to women on social media.

Patricia Scotland (Baroness Scotland) was the first woman to hold the role of Attorney General (over 700 years after the job was created). The Attorney General is the chief legal adviser to the Government in England and Wales. Born in Dominica in the West Indies, she moved to Walthamstow aged two. She became a barrister (a lawyer specialising in court work), and was the first black woman to be appointed Queen's Counsel, which is a senior barrister. She was made a member of the House of Lords (the upper house of parliament) in 1997 and held many jobs in the Labour governments from 1997 until 2010. In 2016 she took up her post as Commonwealth Secretary-General. The Commonwealth is an organisation of over 50 countries who have historic ties with the United Kingdom. She was the first woman to hold this post too!

"How insensitive, inartistic, unscientific, and ungracious it is to take anything for granted!"

— *Muriel Lester*

Social Change

George Monoux was a merchant and Lord Mayor of London who died in 1544. Towards the end of his life he lived in Walthamstow. George was a philanthropist – someone who gives lots of money to good causes – and his projects included a bridge over the Lea Marshes so that people from East London could get into London more easily. He also left money to build the college that is now named after him. Similarly, nearly 400 years ago a rich grocer called **Thomas Gamuel** lived in Walthamstow. When he died he left instructions for his money to be used to provide poor people with bread every week, and he left his land to be used for the good of those living in the area. Some of this land was used in Victorian times to build a school. There is a still a school on the same site, and it is still named after him.

In the 19th century a publisher called **Edward Lloyd** produced many books of popular stories that he sold cheaply so that more people could afford to buy them. This earned him lots of money and he used it to publish newspapers. One of them, which came out on Sundays, was called *Lloyd's Weekly*, and each copy was read by over a million people. He also created the newspaper the *Daily Chronicle*, which was known for having news from all over the world. He loved new technology and used the latest printing techniques for his papers, as well as making sure he owned the resources to make paper and ink (economists call this vertical integration). After he died his son Frank gave Edward's house and its gardens to be used for local people – it was opened as Lloyd Park in 1900.

In May 1882 **Queen Victoria** visited Epping Forest to dedicate it to the people. She arrived at Chingford Station by train before travelling by carriage to High Beach in Essex. The station was decorated with thousands of flowers and a sign saying 'The Forest Welcomes the Queen'.

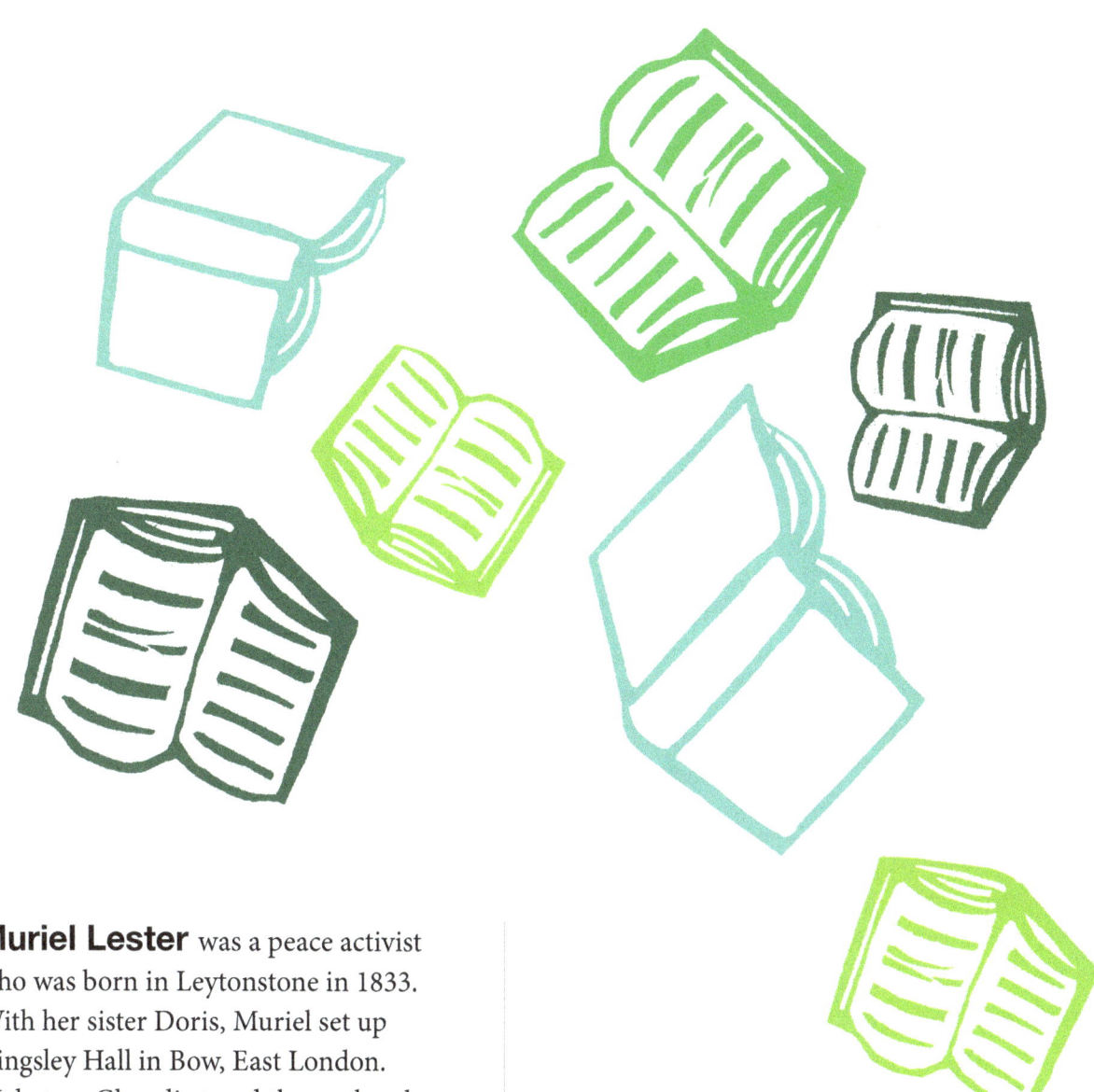

Muriel Lester was a peace activist who was born in Leytonstone in 1833. With her sister Doris, Muriel set up Kingsley Hall in Bow, East London. Mahatma Ghandi stayed there when he visited London for a conference on the future of India. He led the campaign for Indian independence and became known throughout the world for his views on peaceful protest. He wanted to stay amongst real Londoners rather than be treated like a VIP in a hotel. Three years later Muriel accompanied Ghandi on his tour of Bihar, India, on his anti-untouchability tour which sought equality for all Indians. Muriel was a pacifist - someone who believes that all war is wrong - and was twice nominated for the Nobel Peace Prize.

Sol Plaatje was a founder and the first General Secretary of the South African Native National Congress (SANNC) political party, which became the African National Congress (ANC). A talented linguist, Sol could speak many languages, including his mother tongue, Tswana, into which he translated some of the works of William Shakespeare. He became a journalist, editor, novelist, and campaigner, and it was while living in Leyton in 1914 -15 that he wrote his influential book, *Native Life in South Africa*.

Social Change

Four people with a Waltham Forest connection have been awarded the Victoria Cross, the highest medal that can be awarded in the British military. It is awarded for gallantry, which means courageous behaviour in battle.

Jack Cornwell doesn't just have a park in Leyton named after him, he also featured on the Royal Mail's first class stamp to commemorate 150 years of the Victoria Cross in 2006. Jack died aged 16 and was awarded his Victoria Cross posthumously (after death). He had joined the Royal Navy without his parents' permission, and served on a ship called HMS Chester. Everyone around him on the ship died when it came under fire in the Battle of Jutland, a sea battle in World War One, but Jack stayed standing, continuing to await orders while in a very dangerous position. The Scout movement named one of their awards after him. The Cornwell Scout Badge is awarded to members who show courage, endurance and 'high character'. There is also a Tri-Service (Sea Cadet Corps, Army Cadet Force and Air Training Corps) building named after him in East Ham.

George Mitchell went to the same school in Leyton as Jack Cornwell – Farmer Road School. In 1957 the school was renamed George Mitchell School in his honour. In World War Two George single handedly captured an enemy gun emplacement (an area for weapons) even though he was being fired at while he did this.

Born in India to Irish parents, **Patrick Mullane** was a sergeant in the British Army's Royal Horse Artillery and was awarded the Victoria Cross for his actions in the Battle of Maiwand (in present day Afghanistan), during a war that took place there in 1878-1880. Patrick attempted to save the life of another soldier even though the conditions were very dangerous, and later went to fetch water for wounded soldiers, putting his own life at risk. He survived this conflict and died in 1919. His grave, decorated with a Victoria Cross, can be seen in St Patrick's Cemetery in Leytonstone.

Edgar Myles was an Air Raid Warden in Leyton during the Blitz (the heavy bombing of London by German Planes during World War Two). Many years before that he had been awarded two bravery awards in just one year. He was given both the Victoria Cross and the Distinguished Service Order in 1916 for 'most conspicuous bravery' – he had gone onto the battlefield alone while being fired at by the enemy and helped those who were wounded.

In 1914, at the outbreak of World War One, a battalion was founded specifically for footballers who wanted to serve their country. Called the 17th Middlesex (The Footballers' Battalion), 10 players from what was then called Clapton Orient (now called **Leyton Orient**) immediately signed up. They were the first to sign up as a group, and this was recognised by King George V who was the first member of the royal family to attend a Football League match when he came to watch Orient in 1921, at their Millfields ground in Hackney.

Creativity

The design of Yoda, Jedi Master, was the work of **Stuart Freeborn**, a make-up artist from Leytonstone who has been called the 'grandfather of modern make-up design'. Stuart was a fan of horror films and would go home after watching them at the cinema and recreate the looks on himself, sending photographs of these to film studios until finally, after lots of rejection, a new studio hired and trained him. Stuart worked on lots of famous films as well as *Star Wars* including classics such as *2001: A Space Odyssey, Oliver Twist* (the 1948 version), *Dr Strangelove, Murder on the Orient Express* and the *Superman* films.

The 'Master of Suspense', **Alfred Hitchcock,** was a film director born in Leytonstone who made over 50 films including, in 1929, *Blackmail*, the first British 'talkie' (film with a synchronised soundtrack so that you can hear the characters talk). Part of his trademark style was to use the cameras to follow the action the way a human would with their eyes. This makes the film seem more real and increases the viewers' sense of fear when it is a scary film. He has been called the most influential director of all time.

Derek Jacobi is an actor from Leytonstone who has won many awards for his acting on stage and television. One of his later roles has been playing 'The Master' in *Doctor Who* – he says being in this show had been one of his ambitions for many years. Derek went to school in Leyton, and after university he joined the Birmingham Repertory Theatre which is where the famous actor and director Laurence Olivier spotted him and invited him to become a founder member of the National Theatre. Derek lives with his husband in London, and in 2015 he was one of the Grand Marshals invited to lead the Gay Pride March in New York City.

Creativity

In the late 1950s and 1960s Walthamstow School of Art was the place to be if you were young, cool and creative. Designers **Marion Foale** and **Sally Tuffin** both attended the college, and later the Royal College of Art, before they set up their own fashion label, Foale and Tuffin, selling clothes made from bright patterned fabric. They were part of what Vogue magazine called 'Youthquake' – a trend that saw fashion, music and culture look to young people for inspiration instead of trying to copy the more traditional trends from expensive fashion houses in Paris. They were also amongst the first designers to make trousers that were designed for women's shapes and to pair them with a matching jacket. When the Queen needed a mantle (cloak) in 1960 for a ceremony that had only been performed by a man before, Marion's design was chosen to create one suitable for a female monarch. Her design is still used by the Queen today.

Photographer **David Bailey** was born in Leytonstone. David has dyslexia and dyspraxia and he struggled at school. After National Service (when you have to spend some time in the military – the United Kingdom had this from 1939 -1963) he bought a camera and found a job as a photographer's assistant. He started to take photographs of fashion icons and famous people, becoming a celebrity himself and part of the 'swinging sixties' scene. David has also directed TV documentaries and he paints and creates sculptures.

A choreographer is someone who invents, designs and teaches dance routines for performance. **Matthew Bourne** is a choreographer who had some of his schooling in Walthamstow. He didn't start dance training until he was 22, which is late as dancers often start training as children. After his career as a dancer finished, he started to produce and choreograph his own shows. Matthew's productions have toured the world, and he is well known for changing the traditional interpretation of stories to include gay characters, such as making *Swan Lake* about a human man falling in love with a male swan.

"Sometimes you don't know what you've got until you put it in front of an audience"

Matthew Bourne

Creativity

Roger Ascham was a writer and scholar in Tudor England. He was asked to teach Princess Elizabeth Greek and Latin as her tutor before she became Queen Elizabeth I - she was able to speak and read Latin, Italian, French, Spanish and classical Greek. He worked for three monarchs - Edward VI, Mary I and Elizabeth I, and published many writings and poetry, including the first book on archery in English, *Toxophilus* (Lover of the Bow), which sought to make people interested in the sport which had gone out of fashion.

The image of Queen Elizabeth I as a Queen married to her country instead of to a King, was one first presented by the poet **George Gascoigne**, who lived in Walthamstow at the time of her reign in the sixteenth century. One of his works, *The Supposes*, was one of William Shakespeare's influences for his play *The Taming of the Shrew*.

Tom Hood was an author, playwright and magazine editor from Leytonstone. He wrote humorous plays and poems as well as children's books, and became editor of *Fun*, a successful satirical comic (satirical means make fun of politicians and people in the news). His dad, **Thomas Hood**, was also a poet and playwright and a contributor to *Fun*'s rival, *Punch*. He was the author of the famous poem *The Song of the Shirt* which highlighted the poverty of a seamstress living in London, Mrs Biddell, which along with work by people like Charles Dickens, raised awareness of the appalling working conditions for many people at the time.

Madge Gill spent some time in the early years of the 20th century working as a nurse at Whipps Cross Hospital. She was a spiritualist – someone who believes that the spirits of dead people exist and can communicate with living people. After having her children, and surviving a serious illness, she started to draw, creating many pictures that she said were guided by a spirit that she called 'Myrninerest'. Madge is an example of an 'outsider artist' which is an artist who is self-taught instead of going to art school, and who has little contact with the mainstream art world. She died in 1961 but since her death her work has become better known, being displayed in galleries across the world, including an exhibition at the William Morris Gallery in Walthamstow.

Artist **Grayson Perry** won the Turner Prize, considered one of the highest honours in the British art world, in 2003. His artwork includes ceramics and tapestries. He has a female 'alter-ego' called Claire who dresses in flamboyant costumes that he designs himself, with over the top make-up. Grayson had his art studio in Walthamstow for many years and he made an artwork called *The Walthamstow Tapestry* in 2009 which looked at the way people interact with brands throughout their lives.

William Morris was an artist, writer and socialist thinker in Victorian times who helped to make British arts and crafts popular, working to ensure that these skills did not die out. In his lifetime he was most known for his poetry and other writings including a translation of Icelandic sagas, but these days he is often more associated with his textile and wallpaper designs which are still popular today. William valued good design and one of his famous sayings is "have nothing in your house that you do not know to be useful, or believe to be beautiful." He was born in Walthamstow at Elm House, which is now the William Morris Gallery in Lloyd Park.

East 17 were a pop group from Walthamstow. They achieved huge success in the early 1990s. The original line up was **Terry Coldwell, Brian Harvey, John Hendy** and **Tony Mortimer** and they were sold to newspapers as being 'bad boys' and rivals to the clean cut (neat and respectable) boy band Take That. Their bestselling single was *Stay Another Day* which was also the UK Christmas number one in 1994. It was in fact their only UK number one although overall they sold 18 million records in Europe, a million more than Take That. Most of the songs were written by Tony. He had impressed a record company with his material but they said they would only give him a deal if he formed a band. The lead singer was Brian.

By the mid 1990s one of the biggest stories in pop music was the rivalry between two 'Britpop' bands, Blur and Oasis. Britpop was a type of catchy pop music that emphasised a kind of light 'Britishness' as opposed to American grunge music which was heavier, louder and a bit miserable. The songwriter and lead singer of Blur was **Damon Albarn**, who spent the first part of his life growing up in Leytonstone before his family moved to Essex. In 1995 Blur and Oasis released songs on the same day in a race to be number one in the charts, which Blur won with the song *Country House*. This became known as 'The Battle of Britpop'. Damon later formed the 'virtual band' Gorillaz. A virtual band is one where the members are depicted as animated characters. Damon is the only permanent member of Gorillaz and he creates work with many different musicians. They are in the *Guinness Book of World Records* as the world's most successful virtual band.

Music

Known as one of the originators of a type of music known as Asian Underground, which combines Indian classical music with Western electronic music, **Talvin Singh** is a tabla player from Leytonstone. The tabla are drums from the Indian subcontinent (Bangladesh, Bhutan, India, Maldives, Nepal, Pakistan and Sri Lanka). Many musicians producing this kind of sound are the children of immigrants to the United Kingdom, who experience two different cultures at the same time, which comes across in the music. Talvin is also a record producer and he has worked with many successful pop stars as well as winning awards for his own music. His club night in East London, Anokha, is said to have influenced a new generation of musicians.

Michael Nyman is a musician and composer who went to school in Walthamstow. He has written music for many films (known as a score) including a film called *The Piano*, for which he was nominated for many awards. He also writes a lot of music for his own band and has worked with many musicians from around the world, experimenting with different types of music. Michael spent some years working as a music critic writing about other people's music and was one of the first to use the word 'minimalist' about the type of music that focuses on sound rather than meaning, something that he does in many of his own compositions.

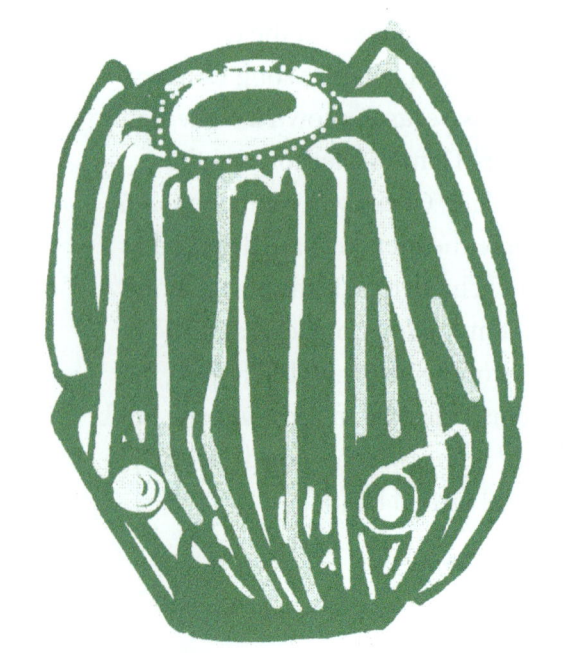

"I'm not a great inventor from scratch. What I do is to use, steal, acquire, reproduce or re-cycle music from other musicians."

— Michael Nyman

Music

Jahmek Power is better known as **Jammer**, a grime MC, rapper and producer. Grime is a type of fast paced electronic dance music that started in East London in the early 2000s. He's a member of the Boy Better Know record label and was part of the original line up of the N.A.S.T.Y Crew, considered the creators of grime. He grew up in Leytonstone and built a music studio in his parents' basement where most of the top grime artists have recorded. He also set up Lord of the Mics where grime artists compete against each other to see whose music gets the best reaction from the audience.

Another grime artist from Waltham Forest is **Lethal Bizzle** (Maxwell Owusu Ansah), from Walthamstow. His single *Oi!* as part of the More Fire Crew was one of the first grime songs to achieve mainstream success and reach the Top Ten in the UK Singles Chart, and he often combines other styles of music with grime. He also came up with the word 'dench' which means something is great or attractive, and has a clothing brand called Stay Dench.

Mandy Parnell is an audio mastering engineer, the person who prepares and transfers recordings of music to a 'master copy' which is the version that is saved and used every time a new copy is made. It is her job to make sure the music sounds the best it can whether you listen to it via an app on a phone or through big speakers in a nightclub or in any other way. She is the founder of Black Saloon Studios in Walthamstow and has worked with many famous artists and won many awards. Her job is not one that many women do and she has said that women have to work particularly hard to prove themselves to the people they are working with. As a young woman she spent some time homeless but after a friend showed her the inside of a recording studio she knew she wanted to work in one and decided to move to London and start studying music production.

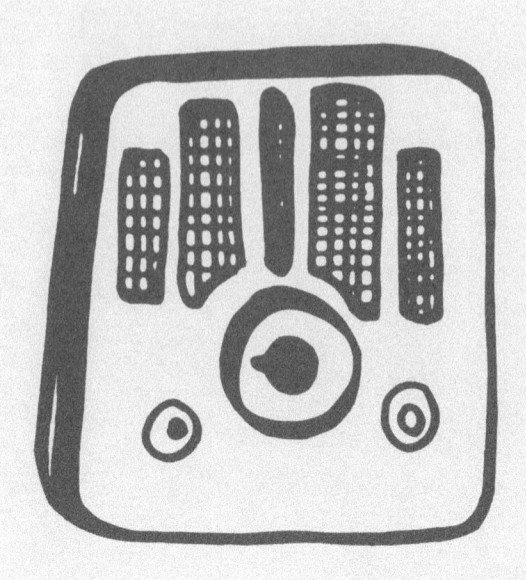

Jazz is a style of music that combines improvisation (coming up with something on the spot rather than writing it in advance) with rhythm (a pattern of different length notes or beats) and melody (the tune). It originated in African-American communities in the late 19th and early 20th centuries, becoming hugely popular by the 1920s. Many jazz musicians have a connection with the borough. **John Dankworth** played saxophone and clarinet as well as composing his own work and writing music for films. He grew up in Highams Park and learnt violin and piano as a boy before choosing the clarinet aged 16 and then adding the saxophone to his list of skills. He used his success in both the United Kingdom and the United States to lead anti-racist campaigns, becoming chair of the Stars Campaign for Inter-Racial Friendship in 1959 when segregation (keeping black people and white people separate) was still going on in much of the United States.

Jackie Free was a musician born in Leytonstone. He played trombone in the Leytonstone Boys' Brigade band, helping them to win many competitions. He played in many famous bands before forming his own, and continued to play gigs well into his eighties.

As well as playing and composing music, **Kenny Wheeler** also arranged music for bands, which means interpreting music other people have written and working out ways of playing it. Originally from Canada, Kenny moved to the United Kingdom in his 20s and spent over 40 years living in Leytonstone. He played trumpet and flugelhorn and although he mostly played jazz he also performed rock music and took part in improvisation sessions.

Born in Leytonstone, **Kenny Clare** was a jazz drummer. He played with many bands and worked alongside many famous singers, including on around 30 number ones in the United States and Europe. Many drummers have said how helpful Kenny was, always happy to discuss drumming technique with other musicians.

Further thinking

Trophies and awards can be given for many things. Design a trophy for someone you know.

Things to think about:

- What is the trophy for? It doesn't have to be for winning a competition. Maybe it is for the person who gives the best hugs or makes the nicest sandwiches.
- What is the trophy made from? Some Trophies are valuable because of the material they are made from. Some are valuable because of what it means to the winner.
- How big will it be? Some trophies are very small even if their significance is big. The Ashes trophy, given to the winner of a cricket competition between England and Australia, is just 15cm tall. It is said to contain the ashes of a burnt cricket bail (one of the pieces of wood that makes up the wicket which is what the ball is aimed at in cricket).

Draw your design here →

A note for teachers and parents/guardians.
Some ideas for lesson plans and further thinking follow on these pages. Please feel free to photocopy any part of this book to use in class or in discussions at home.

Further thinking

Imagine you have been given an award. Who would you thank in your acceptance speech?

Things to think about:
- What is your award for?
- Who has helped teach you the skills that helped you get the award?
- Who has shown you love and encouragement?
- Has anyone made the path to success easier for you? For example maybe somebody historical first helped women access whatever it is you are being awarded for, or introduced the skill or sport to your local area.
- Who would be offended if you do not mention them?

Write your speech here

Further thinking

Thomas Hood wrote *The Song of the Shirt* in 1843 about a woman called Mrs Biddell.
This is the first verse:

With fingers weary and worn,
With eyelids heavy and red,
A woman sat in unwomanly rags,
Plying her needle and thread –
Stitch! Stitch! Stitch!
In poverty, hunger, and dirt,
And still with a voice of dolorous pitch
She sang 'The Song of the Shirt!'

Write a poem about any of the people working in your local area.

Things to think about:
- Do they wear a uniform?
- What noise do they make?
- What tools or equipment do they have?
- Do they seem to enjoy their work?

Brainstorm a list of words here:

Further thinking

Write your poem here:

Further thinking

Rewrite your poem from the perspective of the person doing the job. So instead of saying 'she does this' or 'he does this' change the point of view to 'I', and think about how they feel rather than how they look to others.

Further thinking

Write an acrostic poem, using the letters from the person's name or job title to begin each line.

- Which of these three types of poem do you like best?

Further thinking

How are you going to change the world?

Things to think about:
- What would you like to invent?
- How could you make society fairer?
- What inspires you to make art or music?
- What sports are you good at?
- What stories do you want to tell?

Further thinking

Lots of councils mark places where extraordinary people lived or worked with a plaque on the wall.

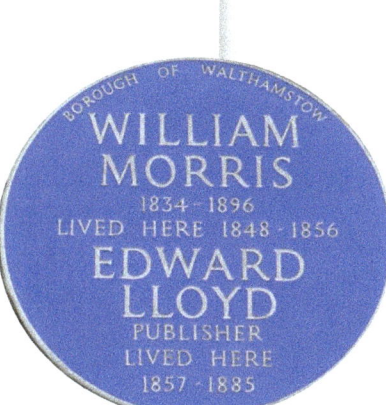

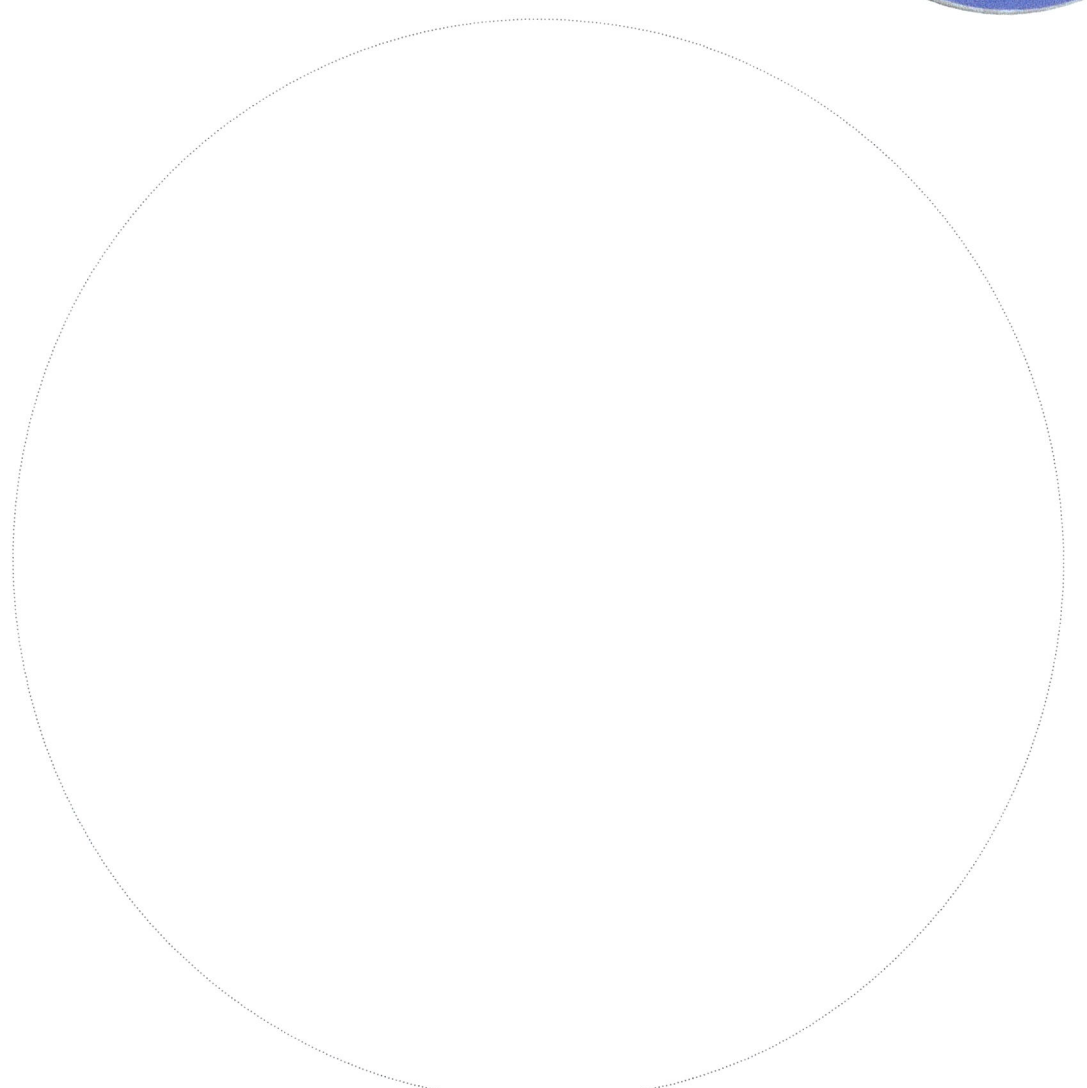

Design your own plaque.

Things to include:
- Your name
- Your year of birth
- What extraordinary thing you are going to achieve

Eleanor and Farah both grew up in Waltham Forest, although they went to different schools and did not meet until they were adults.

They both love the fact that in Waltham Forest you can meet people from all over the world who have made the borough their home, and experience culture and try foods from all over the world.

Eleanor's favourite spots in Waltham Forest are the Hunting Lodge in Chingford and its views over Epping Forest, Walthamstow Market for the bargain hunting and different voices that you hear, as well as all of the spots that let you glimpse the London skyline in the distance.

Farah's favourite spots in Waltham Forest are the picnic table on Walthamstow Marshes near Coppermill Lane, watching the trains zip past the barriers at the signal crossing in Highams Park, and Hollow Ponds on Leyton Flats for boating and duck feeding.

This book is dedicated to their children, V, C, L and A, who are all extraordinary.

We Are Extraordinary was originally supported by Waltham Forest Council as part of the London Borough of Culture 2019.